# E- PUBLISHING MADE EASY

Do-it-yourself Steps to Publishing your E-book On Amazon

## Tabitha Gbuyiro

© 2021, Tabitha Gbuyiro, E-Publishing Made Easy. All rights reserved.

No part of this book may be reproduced, scanned or distributed in any printed, mechanical or electronic form (including recording or photocopying) without written permission, except in the case of brief quotations embodied in critical articles or reviews. Note that neither the author nor the publisher shall be liable or responsible for any loss or damage allegedly arising from any information or suggestions in this book.

All rights reserved for translation into foreign languages.

For information on quantity discounts or having this title customized for your company, please email tabithagbuyiro05@gmail.com.

Requests for permissions should be addressed to tabithagbuyiro05@gmail.com. Or marksontherockpublications@gmail.com

I dedicate this book to Abba Father, the Father of the Fatherless, my refuge and strength, the one who keeps ordering my steps according to His own purpose and who has not stopped His wonders in me by showing up in diverse ways and turning me to His channel through which other lives can be impacted.

## ACKNOWLEDGEMENTS

Firstly, I thank God for calling me into the ministry of helps as a scribe, it's been a journey of total reliance on His spirit of wisdom and I say, all glory goes to Him alone.

I consider it a rare privilege to work with great minds on this project. I want to start by thanking Victor Olatunji for giving me a befitting cover page, I pray for yet greater wisdom for greater works. I will like to register my gratitude to my sister from another Mum, Laide Adeyemo for being a shoulder I could always lean on, the Lord bless you beyond your wildest imaginations. I cannot but deeply appreciate the Amazon team that selflessly trained and provided me with all the supports needed to build the right foundation for this project, God bless and expand you on every end. Special thanks to Oluwaseun Badejo for agreeing to write a superb foreword for this book and helping with editing as well as giving the project a professional touch despite your busy schedule, your contribution to this project is a great boost of courage and confidence to me, the Lord shall yet increase you. Thank you Ibukun Mochiah for your selfless support throughout the project, your profiting in life and ministry shall appear to all. This project would not have been a success if I do not have the backing of my darling husband, you have been my motivator and power house always striving to see me get better at the things that I do, your light shall continue to shine. I say a big thank you to my children for giving me space to bring this project to fruition. I sincerely appreciate everyone that knew about this project and prayed for me or encouraged me at one point or the other, your contribution is marked in eternity and you cannot escape divine rewards. Thank you all for all you have done, I owe you all.

# FOREWORD

Tabitha Gbuyiro in E-publishing made easy outlines how to take your writing from manuscript to eBook in five easy steps.

The book in its opening chapter emphasizes the importance of giving your book a focus so that it resonates with your targeted audience and keeps you the writer on track to accomplishing your writing goals.

E-publishing made easy will also show you how to format your work, so that it is ready for publishing on Amazon's kindle platform which will bring your work to a global audience and give it the maximum reach possible.

Tabitha in her book also gives useful tips and links on how to procure proofreading and editing services at affordable rates that will polish your work and make it shine and truly standout.

This book will particularly be useful for those who have their manuscripts ready but have kept them locked away because of the often perceived cumbersome process of publishing a book.

Overall E-publishing made easy as the name suggests is a simple-to-use step by step guide that will get you published in record time.

It is well written, concise and straight forward.

I highly recommend it.

Seun Badejo

Author of Everything the light Touches

**CONTENTS**

Introduction: E- Publishing, easier than you thought     1

Chapter 1: Have a Dream     2

Chapter 2: The E-book format     4

Chapter 3: Preparing your manuscript     7

Chapter 4: Formatting your work     12

Chapter 5: Publishing on Amazon     23

## INTRODUCTION

### E-Book Publishing, easier than you thought

Just like the title of this book, to publish that amazing manuscript of yours into an e-book is truly easier than you might have ever imagined. E- Publishing Made Easy is a book borne out of a burden to see the scribal callings of 'the called' fulfilled. I believe very strongly that there's a lot God has released for this season and a heavy scribal oil on this generation and I'm passionate to seeing this accomplished by God's design.

So, this little book is set out to take you through a step by step journey from conceptualising your message to adding the required ingredients to presenting the information acceptably and to the simple do-it-yourself method of getting your book published electronically on Amazon.

You will be motivated to waste no further time to get your message out; just by following the steps outlined with an open mind and being deliberate to take the needed action. Don't be in a hurry while reading this book, it's a practical guide, you will need to follow the steps systematically in order to achieve the desired success on your scribal journey.

I believe by the time you are done with this book, you would be an author already, so I congratulate you ahead!

# CHAPTER ONE:

## Have A Dream.

I will want to first salute your courage to have answered the scribal call. The task of conceptualising a unique message and presenting it to the world carefully and tastefully in order to reach the designated audience is enormous. Either you are a beginner on the scribal journey or you've got your finished manuscripts waiting to be published, you have enrolled on a noble cause.

However, before you present your message to the world, you need to have a dream and also understand why you need to. It is important before embarking on any endeavour to have the end result in sight. Know what you are expecting as the outcome of the book project. Not having a dream for your book project is similar to not finishing a story before performing it on stage. You must know what impact you want your book to have on its readers, you must approach the project with a sense of readiness based on the purpose set for the book. Having a dream for your book project will benefit you in the following ways:

1. **It separates you from the rest:** no two books will have exactly the same desired result. So, having your goals right before you will save you the headache of copying another writer or trying to be like others. It will make you unique and help you to remain your very self all through the project. If you received an idea directly, why do you need to copy someone else to present that same idea to the world? There might have been one thousand books on the same subject, your presentation brings a different light into the matter and that fresh insight is what the world is waiting for.

2. **It is a booster:** when you have a dream for your book project, it will give you the boost you need to carry through. No matter how enthusiastic you were at the inception of a book project, a time will come when you will feel less motivated about it and if care is not taken, that may be the end of that book. Once you lose

the passion for that idea, or you allow other peoples' sentiments on the subject to becloud your ideas, you may end up not bringing that book to life. But when you remember that little girl for whom 'chapter two' was visualized to raise back to her feet after being sexually molested for instance, something wakes you up in the middle of the night and you lose your sleep till you have completed that chapter. That's the power of dreams!

3. **It helps you envision the book as a seed:** imagine the great books you have read. There is no way all the points made in a book can sink into your mind, it's just not possible. But it may just be a few thoughts, concepts or ideas that will resonate and stick. How many times have you read a book, the author is talking about something else but the subject opens up to you in a different way entirely. You see something different from what is written, and that new thing you have seen eventually becomes what germinated to produce a changed lifestyle or perception about a situation you are grappling with.

4. **It keeps your heart fully occupied:** when you have a dream about a book project, it keeps you busy at all times. It becomes your waking and sleeping thought. No space for idleness. You are busy working towards the dream you had about the book. No place for distractions, you are focused on a goal. It helps you to be dedicated and have a sense of responsibility towards the project.

5. **It will keep you enthusiastic throughout the project:** When you set the end result always before you and continuously visualize it, there will constantly be a surge of energy to move on. That's the power of having a dream.

If you don't have your manuscripts yet, I will like to refer you to the twin of this book, ***'Write that Book'***. The book will simplify the writing process, with practical guidelines on how to polish your ideas and ensure that your message gets to your audience and also achieve its purpose. This is the whole essence of writing.

## CHAPTER TWO:

## The E-book Format

### Brief History

In 1971 Michael S. Hart digitized the United States Declaration of Independence, becoming the first eBook. Ever since, the eBook format has continued to gain wide acceptance and by February 2011 eBooks accounted for the greater part of sales from U.S Publishers than any other format, including paperbacks and hardcovers, according to a report from the Association of American Publishers. The eBook format has continued to become increasingly popular and especially in the self-publishing community and by 2018, 1.68 million electronic books were already self-published. (http://govbooktalk.gpo.gov-The History of eBooks from 1930's to today's GPO eBook services).

**What's an E-book?**

An E-book is an electronic version of a book that can be read on or offline via an electronic device i.e; iPads, tablets and smartphones. It is published electronically. It's also known as an electronic book with its publication made available in digital form, consisting of text, images, or both, and readable on the flat-panel display of computers or other electronic devices

Let's look at a few differences between the hard copy (Physical Print) book format and e-books.

| Physical Prints | Electronic Books |
|---|---|
| Has texts, images, etc. printed on paper | Digital text or electronic book |
| Pages are bound together and has either hard cover or soft cover back | Formatted into a file that can be read on an e-reader device or app |
| Has static layouts that do not change once printed | Has dynamic layouts and with reflowable texts |
| Contents are presented with pages attached to direct readers | E-readers search function is used to navigate throughout the book. Pages are not really relevant |

**E-book Distribution**

Usually, e-books are distributed on the internet as downloadable files that can be read offline. It can also be inform of web pages that are cached by a web browser for reading offline.

Generating customers for an e-book requires a great deal of skill and understanding. There are various platforms through which your e-books can be published and sold globally, although this book focuses majorly on selling your books on amazon. It's important to highlight the fact that you could sell your e-books directly on your website. This has its undeniable advantages such as:

1. Giving you the greatest possible control and independence as well as full control of sales.

2. Helping you become an authority on the idea you are presenting to the world

3. It is a way to build engagement with your audience directly without interference.

4. It helps create traffic for your blog as well as an email list from those important contacts who would love to learn directly from you. You could generate a huge number of followers and mentees from this exercise.

However, selling directly will be more rewarding if your website is already well-known and has built appreciable traffic before the publishing project. If you don't have an appreciable following and you don't have the time to wait to build that following, then it will be better to stick to a platform like Amazon first.

Some of the benefits of self-publishing on Amazon includes:

1. You have an opportunity to offer print books for pre-order.

2. It is free.

3. With Kindle create software, you will have your books published without stress.

4. You have the opportunity to print paperback copies too.

5. The Amazon platforms provides sales ranking; which will let you know how many copies of your book have been sold and how well your book is doing.

6. Great reports dashboards are parts of the benefits you enjoy with Amazon; instantaneous sales reports and many other useful insights are accessible through an array of user friendly tools on the Amazon Kindle app.

If you have published your eBook(s) already but you discover that your book sales are low, watch out for my book: **eBook Marketing Without Sweat**; in it you will find useful tips needed to get that book to your prospected audience with ease and with great results.

## CHAPTER THREE:

## Preparing your Manuscript

There are various sections and segments that turn your manuscript into an E-Book, it's important we take a look at them one after the other.

Segments of your book to be converted to e-Book or for normal publication includes the following:

*1. Cover page*

*2. Copyright page*

*3. Dedication*

*4. Acknowledgement*

*5. Foreword*

*6. Table of contents*

*7. Introduction*

*8. Body (or Chapters).*

*9. Back page (blurb/about the author).*

### 1. Cover page

That's the first thing you see in a book, it must be catchy, classy and attractive. Your cover page will depend largely on your audience or the industry you are writing for, so take your time to choose the best design that will go well with your title and make your book attractive at the first sight!

### 2. Copyright ©page

That's the protection and ownership rights to the contents of the book.

**Warning**: please note that the information written in any book in the copyright pages informs the reader the extent to which you can use the contents and who to contact before usage.

Copyright abuse is a great crime. It can cost you money and you may even end up imprisoned. **DO NOT COPY OTHER PEOPLES WORK!** It is called Plagiarism and it's a big crime globally.

Even when you see an idea in a book which you find helpful on your book project, add your own thoughts to it. Research on the same topic and create your air around the same idea. This is very vital. You may want to pass your work through an online plagiarism checker: duplichecker.com, grammarly.com, smallseotools.com, quetext.com (This list is far from exhaustive, you can use the key word *'plagiarism checker'* and see which works for you, some may come at a cost, but be willing to make the investment.

### 3. Dedication

Usually, a book is dedicated to someone that has affected one's life positively in one way or the other. This could be your grandfather, grandmother, father, mother, husband, wife, an uncle, father in-law, mother in-law, aunty, children, etc.

### 4. Acknowledgement

This refers to people that contributed towards the success of the book, this may include but not limited to the editors, the proofreaders, the typist, contributors, advisers, spouse, children etc.

### 5. Foreword

A piece of writing that serves to introduce the reader to the author and the book is called foreword. It is usually written by someone who is not the author or an editor of the book. It could be a renowned author in the area the book covers who is technically qualified to endorse the book. They are meant to boost reception and recognition of the book, the materials used amongst many others.

## 6. Table of Contents

This describes a quick guide for readers to have a lead to a particular chapter. It could also create a touch of flow around the idea to be presented. A creative writer tries to begin the suspense experience right from the table of contents. It's an opportunity to whet the appetite of a reader. It comes with the chapter title and the pages. However, it is important to note that eBooks usually have reflowable texts which makes the pages almost irrelevant as the reader can use search function to navigate throughout the book. Depending on your writing style and your target audience, your chapter titles should not be too flat and archaic. Spice your ideas up with some good titles. Make every chapter a must read.

## 7. Introduction

Your introduction is expected to tell readers in summary what they are about to be exposed to through the book. This is an opportunity for you to captivate your audience. This segment must never be dull. Create an atmosphere of expectation and an eagerness in the reader. To explain the role of an introduction in a book project, I will liken it to the look of a meal being served and then covered with a dirty lid. No matter how great the aroma, look and the eventual taste of the food, except you have a very hungry guest who may not care much about the lid and it's poor appearance, you may end up eating the food yourself! The same thing goes with the introduction of your book. If this segment of your book is poor and shabby, no matter how great your idea is, you will lose a lot of readers immediately.

Note that the best time to write your introduction is not before you pen the full body of the work, rather, it should come last, when you have concluded all the writing, so the introduction serves as a form of summary.

If you write your introduction before finishing your book contents, you may eventually convey an incomplete message in your introduction. Ensure that you have completed the main body of your book before you write your introduction so as to give the right insight into what the book is all about.

### 8. Body

This is also referred to as Chapters or Interior of the book. Here is where you develop the content of the book. You dig into what the book is all about.

You do justice to the subject matter by breaking your ideas or story down into bits and pieces. Ensure clarity and simplicity. You don't want to write a book that readers have to read a sentence about five times before they understand the point you are trying to make. I understand some styles of writing employ the use of complex sentences but even such styles should endeavour to convince and not confuse a reader as much as possible. The body of the book should be the real place where you sell your ideas to the world (your audience or readers of your book). You have to be meticulous about your presentation and the flow of points presented.

### 9. Back Page

Your book can have what is called a **BLURB**. This refers to a short description of your book, usually written at the back of your book.

Blurb can interchangeably be used as "ABOUT THE BOOK" although it's not professional to have the heading "ABOUT THE BOOK" in a book. The standard way is just to go ahead and write the description of your book. You need to be conscious of your audience to ensure that you employ the appropriate language.

Another very important segment of the back page is **"ABOUT THE AUTHOR"**. Here is where a short description about you is being stated. It should be written in the third person format, avoid the use of "I" or "I am". Here is a good example:

Rebecca Badmus is a dynamic Poet and author. She is the co-founder of Silver and Gold Publications etc.

# CHAPTER FOUR

## Formatting Your Work

This is the most technical aspect of your E-book publishing journey, but understand that it is not something complex and you can do it all by yourself. First, you need to know what formatting is in this context.

**What is Formatting?**

Formatting is the layout of your documents in a presentable manner that will be able to pass on a publishing platform, in this case, Amazon.

If your book is to be published on Amazon, you cannot afford to arrange your work shabbily or leave your manuscript without order. There is a standard and the Amazon platform will not accept anything that falls below the acceptable standard. You need to get accustomed to the professional way. You are expected to have a global view, so you must prepare your manuscript following global standards. If you have a ready manuscript just waiting to be published, I charge you to take another look and ask if you are confident your ideas will cut-across different races, ethnic groups, people of various languages and cultures. This is very important.

That required standard is what the next few pages will deal with.

**Good News**

If you know the secrets of publishing books on Amazon, it will be like a piece of cake. Not only would you have conquered what many professional writers are still battling, you will also become the answer to somebody's prayers by becoming a seasoned publisher of their e-books on a platform like Amazon. But before this can be achieved, you must be ready to pay the price, to understand what needs to be done and be diligent enough to follow through on the required standard.

Formatting guides you in preparing your e-book for excellent publishing.

Follow these 10 Do-It-Yourself steps to format your manuscript.

**Note:** The most used trim size in Amazon is 6" x 9". You have to take this into consideration when setting your pages and margins

*Step 1. Set your page and margin.*

*Step 2. Choose suitable styles and customise same.*

*Step 3. Format the interiors - chapters.*

*Step 4. Fix your cover designate*

*Step 5. Pagination*

*Step 6. Headers fixation*

*Step 7. Extras*

*Step 8. Add images if available*

*Step 9. Arrange the Table of Contents*

*Step 10. Proof and conversions to PDF*

Note that all these steps can be achieved using Microsoft word, so relax and get down to work. Like it was stated, it's a Do-It-Yourself approach. The highlight below will guide you through each of the steps in case you are not vast on MS Word.

**Step 1**: To Set Page and Margin

- Go to Home Tab
- Choose the style that fits your write up
- Go to Page layout Tab to set your margin

**Step 2:** To Choose Styles

- Go to Home tab and choose the style that best fits your write up.

**Step 3**: To Format the Chapters

- Go to Home tab
- Locate the paragraph section to set your text and line spacing.

**Step 4**: To fix your cover designate

- This is very easy to create. Mere looking at one or two books can inspire you on the kind of cover designate that will be fitting for your write up.

**Step 5**: For Pagination

- It's expected that you exclude the cover page, copyright page, Abstract, Dedication, Acknowledgements as well as Content page in the general numbering of the pages. You may want to start the real pagination of your book from Introduction, depending on your kind of write up.
- To exclude the first few pages in your pagination exercise, follow the simple steps below:
    - Set the cursor at the beginning of the first word on the page where you want the page numbers to start from
    - Go to Page Layout
    - Click on breaks and scroll to section breaks
    - Click on Next Page (go to home tab to insert paragraph on the document to ensure the section page has been effected. Click the same paragraph button to remove the paragraph sign).
    - Go to Insert Tab
    - Click on Page numbers to choose a paging style and click ok.

- Click on Page numbers again and scroll to format. Go to page numbering and click the start button. Insert 1 in the space provided and click ok.
  By now the whole document would have been numbered including the first set of pages. Don't panic. Follow the rest of the final steps. It's easy.
- Ensure that header and footer of the document is still highlighted. Go to Header and Footer Design, at the navigation section, the 'link to previous' is supposed to be highlighted in blue. Click on it to remove the highlight. (This implies that the two sections created in your document have been detached and can be edited separately).
- From the Page you like the pagination to start, you should be having 1. Then scroll to the first page which is still paginated, highlight the page number and press the delete button. That singular action should remove all the page numbers in the first few pages (section one of your document) which you intended to exclude in your pagination.
- The second section which begins from where you want the pagination to start should have been numbered starting from 1.
  If you have not gotten the result expected, go over the steps again.

**Step 6-9** are extras and things you can easily fix without stress.

**Step 10**: Proofing and Conversion to PDF

- Proof reading your manuscript is very essential as it was clearly stated earlier that no software can replace this function. In addition to this, you will want to conserve your originality as much as possible hence the need to read your work again even after final editing.

- Converting your manuscript to PDF format is the last step to be taken when all changes have been accepted and the manuscript is ready to be uploaded on the kindle app for publishing. To get this done, go to File tab, scroll to export and click. Click on 'create PDF document'. It's that simple!

If you carefully follow these steps, I congratulate you ahead because your E-book is on the way to be published!

**EDITING YOUR MANUSCRIPT**

One aspect of writing that most authors dread is editing. The task of writing is cumbersome enough, so, leaving this aspect to professionals is not anything ambiguous but you will be exposed to a list of apps that can aid you and help you do justice to your manuscript as well as set it to taste for publishing.

There are three basic steps in Editing

*1. Structural edit*

*2. Line edit*

*3. Proofread*

**Who is a book Editor?**

He is interchangeably referred to as a proofreader.

- Checks the structure of your book

- Copy or line edits parts of your book

- Proofread your manuscript

Creating your E-book starts from the use of Microsoft Word to format your document. However, writing and publishing has become lot easier these days with the advent of several tools such as editing apps and links that can effectively aid self-editing for easy self-publishing of your book either electronically or otherwise.

It is however very important for you to understand clearly that **NO SOFTWARE** can replace a human editor or proof reader so, don't trust any of the offered list unconditionally. The aim of this chapter and this practical handbook is to provide you with helpful suggestions and a handy guide that will enhance you in the self-publishing journey of your e-book. It is the right combination of tools that will help you polish your manuscript and give it an outstanding presentation.

**ONLINE TOOLS/APPS AND LINKS FOR EDITING**

**1. ProWriting Aid**

Features

- Easy to use

- Edits for

- Typos
- Grammar mistakes
- Plagiarism

- Improve readability of your writing

- Works well with Scrivener

- Ideal for fiction Authors

**Note**

- Mobile App not available and
- It's not a replacement for a proof reader

## 2. Vellum

<u>Features</u>

- Used to format manuscripts into Kindle, Kobo etc e-Books as well as print books

- It's a great resource to self-publish in stores like Amazon

- It's user friendly

- Allows you drag and drop several chapters of your manuscripts and format the whole book just in an hour!

- Can help assemble series of books

- Allows add store, social media links etc.

- Has great looking book templates

**Note**

- Quite expensive
- Available on Mac only
- Not a replacement for a proof reader

## 3. Grammarly

<u>Features</u>

- It's a top editing tool for writers and authors in varying genres

- Edits for

- Grammatical mistakes
- Typos
- Plagiarism

- Has a dedicated style guide

- Works everywhere via plugins, add-ons, etc

- Free versions are available

- Works well with MS Word

- Has dedicated apps for Android, IOS, Apple, Mac

**Note**

- Not built with Novelists in mind because it won't allow you paste a whole book at once
- Best suited for non-fiction writers
- Not a replacement for human editor or proof reader

## 4. Scrivener

Features

- Good for self-editing before hiring an editor

- Allows setting of a custom status for individual chapters e.g first draft or final read etc.

- Can move different parts of the book

- Easy to view the status of each chapter of the book before sending to an editor

- Minimises distractions during editing by hiding desktop and presenting only your manuscript

- Ideal for large projects

**Note**

- Requires customization,
- You may need some time to learn to use all its features effectively
- It is not a replacement for human editor

## 5. SmartEdit

Features

- It's a rare online tool highly suited for Novels and short stories

-Edits for

- Misused words
- Misspelled words
- Misused Adverbs and Phrases
- Repetitive words and phrases
- No need to drop the text sections after the other
- You can run your manuscript through all at once
- Spots flaws when reviewing a draft

**Note:**

- Meant for word only,
- It has less options and suggestions than Grammarly

## Helpful Online Editors

### 1. Hemingway Editor

- Free writing and editing software: all you need do is paste your chapters in one by one

- Helps to identify adjectives and adverbs that should be out

Generally, your book becomes more appealing to a reader when all the unnecessary words have been cut off.

### 2. GoogleDocs

- It's a draft online editor for collaborative writers

- Includes revision history

- Backs up automatically

**3. Grammarly web app**

- Useful for revising drafts on the go

- Can set writing goals like word counts, tone of voice or style

- You can even improve your writing skills with the premium version of this app

- The business version possess features for larger writing projects

-This app includes a handy custom dictionary

For a human editor and proofreader; you may book a free consultation by sending an email with a sample of your work to Primepublishingconsult@gmail.com.

Publishing on Amazon is truly an amazing experience. You don't want to trade this for anything, so make up your mind that you will see through to the end of your book project, and you will do it yourself because if I can, then you can!

You can either have your e-Book (Digital Publication) or paperback publication. Another exciting thing here is that you can publish the two simultaneously on Amazon. e-Book first, followed by paper back immediately.

**PAPERBACK**: This is also known as a softcover or softback. It is a type of book characterized by a thick paper or paperboard cover, and often held together with glue rather than stitches or staples.

Paperback editions of books are issued when a publisher decides to release a book in a low-cost format. It's the hardcopy version of your e-book, while the digital publication is the softcopy of the same book.

However, it is easier to go through the amazing Amazon app to get your softcopy in less than 3 days (with all the support features from the application), and then proceed to produce same as hardcopy. This is a very cheap, economical and yet a quality based process. It brings you at par with professionals who spend milions to get their books to the public; this is what makes the Amazon platform amazing

Imagine producing 500 copies of a 300 page book for ₦1.5M and compare that with having the opportunity to produce a soft copy and paperback of the same manuscript on Amazon for free. After so many years, your book on Amazon will still earn you money. Without spending a dime for a local printer or a publishing house, you are being presented with a privilege to earn for life through Amazon.

That is the basic difference between manual labour (manual book printing) and the digital work space. Which will you consider cost effective for you?

## CHAPTER FIVE:

### Publishing on Amazon

This chapter will lead you step by step on how you can open a kindle direct publishing account on Amazon and get your book out without stress. This is where we dive into the reality of publishing.

To set up your own account, you will need the under listed items:

1. A Smart phone

2. Data

3. A computer system

Follow the steps below:

**Step 1. Sign up.**

Copy the following link on the browser of your smart phone. https://kdp.amazon.com/en_US/. A form will prop up.

**Step 2. Fill the form:** Be careful with everything you are filling. Make sure the information is correct because the details you give will determine where your cheque will be sent to.

Go to your account and fill in the necessary information. Click on each box, and answer, one after the other. Ensure your address is correct.

After you have successfully opened your account, the next stage is how to get paid.

**Step 3. Fill in your Bank details**: Opt for Cheque payment, except you have a bank account in the US.

Amazon.com which pays in dollars, not UK or other options provided.

If you have a Payoneer account, it will give you an option aside from cheque for payment.

(You can check this out @www.payoneer.com).

**Step 4. Tax information**: This is commonly referred to as Tax Interview.

Ensure you fill in your details accurately. Deselect "I have a Non-US TIN", then choose the option: "The country where I am liable...doesn't issue TIN"

Click on "Continue"

**Step 5. Move on to "Sign and Submit"**

You will be asked to "consent or not" to having an electronic signature. It's advisable to consent, otherwise, you will always have to append your signature on hard copies of documents that will be despatched to you.

Afterwards, fill in your names, exactly as you had done at the upper part of the form.

Read through the Certificate issued to ensure your details are accurate before submission.

Finally, you will be directed to a page that will show that the Tax information interview has been validated. Then you can Exit Interview.

Having your Kdp account means; you can now publish your eBook as soon as your manuscript is ready.

Let's go through the following steps to get your eBook out there.

**Step 1**: Under "**Create a New Title**", select "**+Kindle eBook**". You will be taken to a three-page set up to create your Kindle eBook.

**Step 2**: Fill in your "**Kindle eBook details**". Here, you will be required to do a few things. It's all easy just like filling a Google form.

- Select language for your book

- Enter your books title and sub-title

- Specify whether your book is part of a series. If it is, type in your series and the number in the series you want to publish at the moment.

- Enter your Author name and names of any other contributor(s) e.g co-author or the person that wrote your foreword.

- Put in a book description. You can use the HTML editor which makes it easy to format your book description. All you need do is copy from the HTML pane to Kdp book description field.

- Include a clear CTA (call to action) at the end. Use a heading tag to give it a distinct outlook and help grab and hold unto your target readers' attention.

- Fill in the publishing rights by selecting "I own the copyright and hold the necessary publication rights".

- Add some keywords. You can add up to seven keywords on Kdp. You must make the most of this opportunity so as to make it easy for Amazon browsers to find your book. Kdp Rocket will assist you to fish out the key words that's most appropriate for your book.

- Choose two Amazon categories for your book. To know the category to choose, look out for other categories similar to your genre that are already doing well in the market.

- Indicate the age or grade range if your book falls into the 'for children' category.

- Choose whether or not you want your book to be released immediately you publish or you want a pre-order period. If you choose a pre-order option, this means your book won't be available until the release period ends, but your book will be visible to book browsers. People can pre-order for the price set and you will have enough time to create a buzz before the launch of your book.

- Click on "**save and continue**". You will be taken to the next page.

**Step 3**: Add your "**Kindle eBook Content**". Here's where you'll upload the content for your eBook.

- Choose '**No**' for whether you want DRM protection or not. This is because the 'Yes' option may deny legitimate buyers access to your book.

- Upload your eBook manuscript. You can use the '**Kindle create**' to convert your eBook's interior file to MOBI format which is the format Kindle uses. You can also use Word, HTML, ePUB etc. which are also accepted by Kdp.

- Upload your "**Kindle eBooks Cover file**" in JPG format. It's advisable to engage the services of a Graphic designer to create a book cover that speaks about the title of your book.

You can also check *fiverr.com,* where you will get highly affordable yet excellent Graphic designers who will deliver on time.

- As soon as Kdp finishes the compilation of your eBook with the interior file and cover page, you are to "**Launch the Previewer**" to see how your book will look like on Kindle. You also need to scan it to fish out any formatting issues.

- Kdp will allow you download a preview to your computer or Kindle device. This will allow you see how your book will look on the kindle e-reader or kindle app if it's published as it is. Approve this copy on Kdp if it's okay. Click save and continue. You will be taken to the third page.

**Step 4**: Set your "**Kindle eBook Pricing**"

Here, you need to choose if you would enroll your book into "**Kdp select**". Enrolling on Kdp select means:

- Your book is exclusive to Amazon and this offers you promotional opportunities and greater visibility during the first 30 days of a 90 day period.

- Your book will be available to Kindle unlimited subscribers.

- You have the chance to earn extra money from their "page reads". If you are a new self-published author, it's advisable you choose this "**Kdp select**" option.

- Choose whether you hold distribution rights for all or just for specific individual territories.

**Note:** if you are the author and this is your first publication, you have world wide distribution rights. This means buyers around the globe can order your book.

- Set your pricing

Here, you'll have the opportunity of seeing what royalty you will earn per sale at that price.

*Note*: *for royalties up to 70%, price must be within the range of $2.9 - $9.99. Any price outside this range will attract a royalty of 35%.*

- Choose whether or not to enroll in Kindle Matchbook. Enrolling means:

- Readers who buy your print book will have opportunity to buy your Kindle eBook at a cheaper rate or to even download for free depending on your choice.
- You also have an opportunity to decide if you want to allow Kindle Book Lending or not. This means that those who buy your book will be able to lend to others within the first 14 days.

- Click save and continue. You will be taken to the third page which is the last page.

Step 5: Click **Publish**!

- You will need to agree to the terms and conditions at the base of this last page

- Confirm that you understand rights and responsibilities.

- Save your book as a draft to publish later or click "**Publish your kindle eBook**".

- If you are publishing right away, a window will pop up that will inform you that your book will go live on Amazon within 72hours(except there is a problem).

Congratulations!

www.ingramcontent.com/pod-product-compliance
Lightning Source LLC
Chambersburg PA
CBHW050307220526
45465CB00002B/860